Adilah's Avocado

Written by Amy Mazzuca

Illustrated by L.E. Webb

Text copyright 2020 by Amy Mazzuca

Illustration copyright 2020 by L.E. Webb

All Rights Reserved.

This is a work of fiction. All names, characters, places and incidents are products of the author's and illustrator's imaginations or are used fictitiously. Any resemblance to actual people, living or dead, events or locales is entirely coincidental.

ISBN: 9781081558406

Acknowledgments

A first book requires many thanks...

To God, who gifted me with the ability to write stories.

To the children in Haiti who call The Welcome Home Children's Centre their home.

To Leslie, who captured my vision with her beautiful illustrations.

To my family for their endless love and encouragement.

Thank you.

- A.M.

To my family, for the hugs and for feeding me!

To Amy, for going on this adventure with me.

To everyone who said "That's awesome! Let me know when it's done. I want to see your art."

- L.E.

Although quite little, Adilah had big ideas. Her ideas were bigger than her huge avocado-shaped eyes. Her ideas were much larger than the small country of Haiti where she lived.

Adilah's eyes were even the colour of an avocado. Not the brown-green colour of the ripe, bumpy avocado skin and not the creamy green colour of the fleshy inside of the avocado. Adilah's eyes were the colour brown, much like the avocado pit.

Even Adilah's favourite food was avocados. "Vitamin rich," Grann would say as she cut around it to expose the pit. Chopped up, drizzled with lime juice, added to mango, and sprinkled with salt and pepper, avocado made a delicious snack.

Together Grann and Adilah shared one last avocado. Adilah held her eyes tight, squeezing out the tears. She thought about the great plane that would fly her over to Canada, her new home, far away from all she ever knew. It had been just a few years since the horrible earthquake that took both her momma and poppa away.

"A better life," Grann told Adilah through the tears that streamed down both their cheeks.

How could anything be better than Haiti? Adilah thought.

Grann reached over and gave Adilah's hand a reassuring squeeze. She told her that no matter where they were, God would be with them. Adilah promised that whenever she felt the warm sun on her face, she would think of her first home, and all the warmth and love that began her life in Haiti. Grann told Adilah that whenever she looked up into the heavens or walked along the roads and saw the familiar zaboka trees laden with avocados, she would think about Adilah, remember her avocado eyes and pray that all would be well. They ended their time together with Grann praying, "Thank you, God, for New Mum who blesses me with hope and Adilah with a future."

Before leaving, Adilah had an idea. Grann agreed and handed Adilah a mesh bag holding one lime, one mango and one avocado, just enough fruit to make a Haitian avocado salad to share with her new mum. "Remember to keep the pit and plant a little bit of Haiti in Canada," Grann said as she tearfully hugged Adilah goodbye.

While on the plane to Canada, Adilah thought about how things would be different. Different because Grann was staying in Haiti and New Mum was in Canada. Different because Grann was black like her, and New Mum was white with yellow hair and green eyes.

Adilah smiled, mindful that New Mum's eyes were green like the creamy inside of the avocado.

Almost a year before, New Mum had come to Haiti looking for ways to help. She stayed there for months giving orphan children a new home, and became a new mum to so many. "Grann is getting older and she wanted me to have a good life, away from hunger and sickness, and so she is sending me to live with New Mum," Adilah told the kind flight attendant as she squeezed her hand tightly. In Adilah's other hand she held the mesh bag of Haitian fruit, stamped with a colourful symbol showing they passed the travel test.

Adilah didn't want to look out the window and watch the ground give way beneath the plane and the rolling hills slowly melt away into the sea, but that is exactly what happened. As she flew, she imagined she was still in Haiti.

Closing her eyes, she brought herself back to Tent City, to the warm brown dirt beneath her feet, where she danced through her days, skipping and spinning around and around until she fell exhaustedly into Grann's arms.

As she dreamed, her feet felt the long walks to collect water, her ears heard the wild howls of the long nights, and her stomach waited the long days for something to eat. Those long waits – that was the only thing Adilah didn't like about Haiti.

She woke up to see a plate of two cookies and a drink of milk set on the tray in front of her. Thinking of Grann, Adilah looked down at her lap and at the mesh bag of Haitian fruit. Her thoughts moved to Canada just as the plane was beginning to land.

New Mum was waiting at the airport in the Arrivals area. Adilah tried to look happy. She tried to appear excited, but she was nervous. She clutched the mesh bag tightly and clung to the kind flight attendant's hand as they made their way toward the customs gate. Adilah's ears buzzed with new sounds, unfamiliar voices and foreign languages. Her eyes darted back and forth, taking in the new surroundings.

The flight attendant had filled out a customs form for the fruit to show the customs agent when Adilah landed. When they got to the desk, the agent asked her what fruit she had with her. Adilah showed him her bag, and explained what she was going to do with it. He thought for a moment, and then said it posed no risk to Canadian farms and let her through. "Enjoy your new home," he said with a smile.

They walked around the corner, through a set of doors and then out into the Arrivals area. And then, her eyes met New Mum's avocado-green eyes. Adilah saw the warmth in her smile, and remembered the joy and hope she brought to so many children in Haiti. Within minutes, Adilah's feelings of fright turned to peace.

The first thing she did was present New Mum with the mesh bag holding the lime, mango, and avocado. Adilah giggled as she watched a big smile appear on New Mum's face as she bent down to scoop Adilah up and give her a big hug. Approvingly, Adilah looked over at the flight attendant. "Mesi," she said, which meant "thank you" in Creole.

It wasn't long after they arrived home that Adilah taught New Mum how to make the Haitian avocado mango salad. Adilah was surprised when she saw another avocado and lime on New Mum's counter.

New Mum cut the Haitian avocado. She scooped out the silky inside and set the pit aside saying, "We will plant this avocado, Adilah. A little bit of Haiti will grow right here in Canada." Adilah smiled a huge smile as her thoughts travelled back to Haiti and what Grann had said.

New Mum then taught her a new way to eat avocados. Mashed and mixed with garlic and onions and lime, the avocados made tasty guacamole. New Mum cut and handed Adilah the other avocado.

"May I mash it?" Adilah eagerly offered.

New Mum nodded, handing Adilah the fork.

Adilah mashed the avocado while New Mum added a squeeze of lime, a sprinkle of salt, a dash of pepper, a crushed garlic clove and a chopped red onion. The smell of the crushed garlic and chopped red onion danced up Adilah's nose and dripped out of her eyes.

New Mum placed one pit in the centre of the guacamole and the Haitian pit in Adilah's hand. Adilah looked at the two pits. They looked so much alike.

Maybe things won't be so different here after all, Adilah thought.

Together they dipped and ate green-slathered corn chips, carrots and celery, and enjoyed the Haitian salad.

Later that day, Adilah took her Haitian avocado pit outside and planted it deep in the earth.

She waited and watered, and
waited and watered, and
waited and
watered,
and…

After nothing happened for six weeks, Adilah dug into the warm, moist soil.

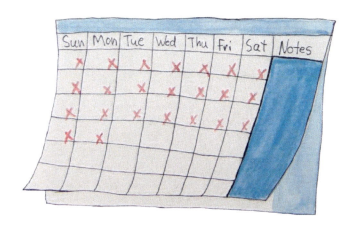

A horrible smell arose from the dirt and she could see the squishy, blackened avocado pit. Horror swept across her face. She choked on the tears and the smell, and carried that pit as far from her nose as her arms would let her. New Mum found her sitting on the back step, a troubled look in her teary eyes. She sat down beside Adilah. Adilah moved close to New Mum and leaned against her.

"Sometimes I close my eyes and feel the sun on my face, and I imagine I am in Haiti. I miss Grann." New Mum wiped the tears that fell.

"I know, Adilah. I know," said New Mum. "Come with me. I have something I want you to see."

Together, hand in hand, they walked down to the market. Once there, New Mum brought Adilah to a counter, and looking up she saw a mound of avocados and smiled. Looking around, she saw more fruit, more vegetables, more food than she had ever seen at one time back in Haiti. Adilah smiled, wishing Grann could also be there.

"Let's try again, Adilah."

Reading the sticker on the avocados, Adilah said,

"These are not from Haiti. These are from Mexico!"

"Remember the pit, Adilah? On the inside, we are all the same."

Adilah remembered the pit and smiled. "You are right, New Mum. We are all the same on the inside."

Together they chose avocados.

One, two, three, ripe and ready.

One, two, three, to ripen for another day.

Once back home, New Mum and Adilah tried a new avocado recipe.

New Mum and Adilah laughed together as they looked at each other, and then in the mirror at the slimy green masks they wore. For the first time, they looked quite a bit alike. Together they laughed and danced around the kitchen until they were out of breath.

Afterward, they sat down together at the computer and researched how to grow an avocado tree.

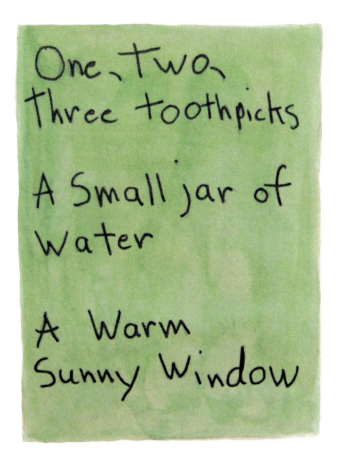

One, two, three toothpicks

A small jar of water

A warm sunny window

More waiting, Adilah thought.

Every morning, Adilah checked on the pit.

"In time," New Mum would say.

Every afternoon, Adilah checked on the pit.

"Trust," New Mum would say.

Every night, Adilah checked on the pit.

"Patience," New Mum whispered.

After five weeks of waiting, the avocado pit began to bulge. Within another week, a tiny sprout erupted through the pit. When it did, Adilah jumped high into the air, let out a shriek of joy and ran to tell New Mum. Together they celebrated by dancing around the tiny zaboka sprout until they grew tired and fell into each other's arms, laughing.

The End

Amy lives in Georgetown, Ontario, with her family and a menagerie of pets. Her greatest passion as a writer is to create lively and engaging stories with vivid word pictures that enrich the lives of readers of all ages. This is her first children's picture book. 100% of her profits will be donated to The Welcome Home Children's Centre in Haiti.

L.E. Webb, a graduate of Sheridan College's Visual and Creative Arts program, firmly believes that the world is a wondrous and often mysterious place. From the light and shadows seen on a sunny afternoon in autumn to the infinite worlds inside the mind; whimsy, memory, observation and a love of storytelling all inspire her to create art. Through painting, drawing, photography, and mixed media, she explores the world around her, hoping that her work will give others a glimpse into the wonders she perceives.

Made in the USA
Monee, IL
01 October 2020